WEEKLY READER BOOKS presents

# What Makes Day and Night?

## A **Just Ask™** Book

Hi, my name is Christopher!

D0003891

Original title: Why Is It Dark?

*by* Chris Arvetis
*and* Carole Palmer

*illustrated by*
James Buckley

NEWFIELD
PUBLICATIONS
MIDDLETOWN, CT.

Dear Parent,

In <u>What Makes Day and Night?</u> your child will learn that Earth rotates as it travels around the sun, resulting in daytime and nighttime. To demonstrate this concept, wise Mrs. Owl and Christopher use a ball, a flashlight, and a big X. The X marks the spot! What spot? Turn the page to find out.

Sincerely,

*Rita D. Gould*

Managing Editor

## FAMILY FUN

- Reenact with your child Mrs. Owl's demonstration of Earth's rotation and orbit. First, on the ground outline a path representing Earth's orbit. Next, role-playing the sun, your child can shine a flashlight on you (role-playing Earth) as you rotate and orbit the sun. Then reverse positions and try the reenactment again.

- Using a large sheet of paper, help your child draw pictures of activities he or she does when it is day and activities he or she does when it is night.

## READ MORE ABOUT IT

- *What Are Seasons?*
- *What Is the Moon?*

This book is a presentation of Weekly Reader Books.
Weekly Reader Books Offers book clubs for children
from preschool through high school.
For further information write to: Newfield Publications, Inc.,
4343 Equity Drive, Columbus, Ohio 43228

This edition is published by arrangement
with Checkerboard Press, Inc.

Weekly Reader is a federally registered trademark
of Weekly Reader Corporation.

Or, to look at it another way, just imagine this...
When it is daytime where Christopher lives, it is dark on the other side of the world, where another mouse will be fast asleep.